THE PENGUINS

BY
LYNN M. STONE

EDITED BY
DR. HOWARD SCHROEDER
**Professor in Reading and Language Arts
Dept. of Elementary Education
Mankato State University**

**PRODUCED AND DESIGNED BY
BAKER STREET PRODUCTIONS**
Mankato, MN

CRESTWOOD HOUSE
Mankato, Minnesota

LIBRARY OF CONGRESS CATALOGING IN PUBLICATION DATA

Stone, Lynn M.
  The penguins.

  (Wildlife, habits & habitat)
  "Baker Street Productions."
  Includes Index.
  SUMMARY:

ISBN 0-89686-326-3

International Standard Book Number:	**Library of Congress Catalog Card Number:**
Library Binding 0-89686-326-3	

ILLUSTRATION CREDITS:

Cover Photo: Kevin Schafer/Tom Stack & Associates
M.P. Kahl/DRK Photo: 4, 8, 13, 14, 24-25, 26, 29, 35, 38, 41, 42
Lynn M. Stone: 7
Kevin Schafer/Tom Stack & Associates: 10
Bob Williams: 17, 32
Al Giddings/Ocean Images, Inc.: 19, 45
Sue Mattews/DRK Photo: 20, 22

CRESTWOOD HOUSE

Hwy. 66 South, Box 3427
Mankato, MN 56002-3427

TABLE OF CONTENTS

Penguins are found only in the Southern Hemisphere. This is a King penguin.

INTRODUCTION:

The word "penguin" was probably first used for the great auk, a black and white sea bird of the North. It was flightless, and it stood erect, just as penguins do. Seamen from Europe saw the great auk on their fishing and whaling journeys. They had known of the great auk for years when it became extinct in 1847.

When the Europeans first discovered penguins in the Southern Hemisphere, the birds reminded sailors of the black and white auks of the North. In those days yet, the black and white birds in the North were still called "penguins," not auks. The explorers thought the black and white birds in the South must be penguins, too. Northern "penguins" later were called auks, but the name "penguin" stuck for the Southern birds, our penguins of today.

The great auk's living relatives, like the auks, auklets, and puffins, look and act something like penguins. They are mostly black and white, stand upright, and use their wings to swim under water. But unlike penguins, the auk family of birds can fly. (The great auk was the only flightless member of the group, a fact which helps explain why it became extinct.) The auk family's wings have not changed into flippers. Auks and their kin are found only in the Northern Hemisphere.

In this book we're going to study the black and white birds that cannot fly.

CHAPTER ONE:

There are eighteen kinds, or species, of penguins. Penguins belong to a family of birds known to ornithologists, scientists who study birds, as *spheniasciformes*. Penguins are the only flightless diving birds in the world. There are, of course, other flightless birds. The ostrich is probably the best known. Others include the ostrich-like rhea, emu, and cassowary. But these heavy, long-legged birds are built for running. Penguins are short-legged. Runners they aren't!

Penguins do have wings, but their wings are not large enough to lift them into the air. Penguin wings are somewhat similar in shape to the flippers of sea mammals. But a penguin's flippers, like the rest of the penguin, are covered by tiny feathers. A mammal's flippers are skin-covered.

All the penguin species live on marine, or salt water, animals. They use their sharp beaks to catch fish, squid, and crusty little creatures known as crustaceans. Penguins feed in the sea, diving to hunt prey. Because of their food, they have to live near ocean water.

Not all penguins are birds of the icy Antarctic. The emperor and Adelie penguins live deep in the Antarctic region. The Galapagos penguin, however, lives in a warm climate on the equator, hundreds of miles north of Antarctica. Almost all of the penguin species live along coasts north of the Antarctic and south of the Tropic of Capricorn.

"Penguis" means *"fat"* in Latin, and penguins are plump birds. Their fat, or blubber, helps to protect them in cold climates. The fattest of the penguins is the emperor. Emperors often weigh around ninety pounds (40.5 kg). Other penguins, in warmer areas, weigh as little as two and one-half pounds (1 kg).

These razorbill auks are relatives of the now extinct great auk.

Adult penguins are generally black and white birds, although the pattern and shade of color differ a great deal. Many species have colorful trimming, especially on their heads. A few kinds have long head feathers called plumes.

Other penguin traits are their short tails and their posture. Penguins stand upright, unlike most birds. Their feet are placed low on their bodies. They seem to stand like prairie dogs. They are often compared to little men dressed in starched shirts and black suits.

These small, gentoo penguins live near Port Lockroy, Antarctica.

Old Penguins

The ancestors of modern penguins may go back a very long time. The oldest remains of penguins that have been found are several thousand years old. These penguins were flightless. At some point—no one knows just when—penguins also had ancestors which could fly. For reasons that are not clear, they slowly lost their ability and need to fly. The wings developed into flippers.

The bones of ancient penguins, known as fossils, are very hard to find. But scientists have found enough fossils to know that there used to be more kinds of penguins than there are today. Why so many species became extinct is a mystery. Change in the penguins' environment was probably one reason. Another reason may have been an increasing number of seals and sea lions. Some penguins may not have been able to compete with the sea mammals and catch their share of food. As a result, over many years, their kind disappeared.

The emperor penguin is a large bird. One of the extinct penguin species, however, probably outweighed the emperor by more than three times! That penguin weighed three hundred pounds (135 kg) and may have stood five feet, seven inches (172 cm) tall. This bird would have outweighed most men!

The most unusual penguin

Among the penguins and among birds in general, the emperor *(Aptenodytes forsteri)* stands out. Besides being the largest of the penguins, it is one of the largest of all birds. The emperor is the only bird in the world that nests somewhere other than on land. It is the only bird that lays its eggs during the Antarctic winter. And the emperor is probably the champion diver among all birds. Because most people think it is the most interesting penguin, the rest of this book will focus on the emperor.

This group of emperors "posed" for a picture at McMurdo Sound, Antarctica.

CHAPTER TWO:

If you travel far enough north you will reach a very cold region. It is the Arctic, home of musk oxen, caribou, and the great white polar bear. The Arctic is an icy, stormy place much of the year. There are long, sunny, summer days, but also long winter days with almost no light. It is one of the toughest places anywhere for creatures to live.

Many people don't realize that if they travel south for a long distance, they will reach an even colder region. This is the Antarctic, home of the flightless bird called an emperor penguin. Like the Arctic, the Antarctic region of the world is icy and stormy. But the Antarctic winter is endlessly long, and the Antarctic summer is very brief and never warm. The Antarctic is an even tougher place for survival than the Arctic.

The mass of land known as the continent of Antarctica is the coldest and windiest continent on earth. Captain Robert Scott, one of the first explorers of Antarctica, called it ''this awful place.''

Antarctica is at the far southern tip of the earth. The imaginary line around the center of the earth is called the equator. The Antarctic region is far south of the equator, at the bottom of the Southern Hemisphere.

Almost the entire continent of Antarctica is covered by a sheet of ice. The ice averages more than one mile,

(1.6 km) thick! Even the Antarctic Ocean, which surrounds the continent, is icebound most of the year. The tremendous shelf of ice around Antarctica may extend five hundred miles (800 km) out over the sea. Each winter the sea freezes up to ten feet (3 m) deep as far as 125 miles (200 km) from shore.

Antarctica is a rugged world of mountains, snow, and ice. Cliffs of blue ice meet darker blue ocean. The night sky glows with streaks of color, called the strange aurora australis. It can be beautiful. Antarctica can also be terrible. The average monthly temperature, even during the summer, never rises above freezing, which is 32° Fahrenheit (0° C). Hurricane winds rush from the mountains and glaciers into valleys and across fields of ice. Frank Debenham, an early explorer of Antarctica, said it was ''the home of the wind.''

Only two or three percent of Antarctica's land surface is not covered by ice. On that exposed, rocky ground, almost nothing can live. Because Antarctica is so cold, very little ice melts. Almost all of the continent's fresh water is locked up, frozen in the huge rivers of ice that are glaciers. With almost no open ground or fresh water, plant and animal life is not very plentiful. For living things, Antarctica is actually an icy desert. There are only a few tiny plants, like mosses, algae, and lichens.

The animal life of the Antarctic continent itself includes perhaps ten kinds of birds and the Weddell seal. The birds nest in Antarctica and the Weddell seal is usually found near shore. Sometimes it crawls onto land.

Other animals like the killer whale and the blue whale live in the ocean nearby.

The amount of ice in the seas around Antarctica changes with the season. Some ice always stays near the continent. In the coldest months the ice shelf rings the continent like a wide, flat necklace. The coastal temperatures are milder than the temperatures of the land itself. Along the Antarctic coast, winter temperatures rarely drop below minus 58° Fahrenheit (−50° C). Summer temperatures can reach 60°-65° Fahrenheit (15-20° C).

These Adelie penguins warm themselves in the summer sun on Torgersen Island, Antarctica.

It is along the coasts, either on the ice or in the sea, where most Antarctic animals live.

The emperor penguin leads a remarkable life. It is the only bird in the world that never needs to come ashore. It can, and sometimes does, move from the sea or ice onto land. But many emperors never touch land. Emperors mate on the ice, and they are born on the ice in the dark Antarctic winter. They fish in the ocean, then crawl back onto the ice. They are truly birds of the cold Southern ice and seas. The emperor is an amazing bird, not only because of how it lives, but because of where it lives.

Most penguins are birds of the ice and snow.

A large bird

Emperor penguins are the largest penguins. They are much larger than king penguins *(Aptenodytes patagonicus)*, their closest relatives. Kings weigh about thirty-five pounds (16 kg), less than half of what a fat emperor weighs.

Animals that live in the coldest climates on earth tend to be bigger than similar animals living in warmer climates. Emperor penguins are larger than king penguins, for example, and they live in a colder climate. Indeed, emperors average about sixty-six pounds (30 kg) and one captured bird weighed just over one hundred pounds (46 kg). Emperors measure about thirty-nine inches (100 cm) from bill to tail. They stand up to forty-two inches (108 cm) tall.

Emperors and kings are the most colorful of penguins. At a glance they look very much alike. Both have shiny white chests brushed with yellow. The yellow is deeper in kings. Both have dark, bluish-black backs and heads that are mostly black. Both have bright patches on the sides of their heads, the emperor's yellow and the king's bright orange. The king also has a brighter orange streak under its lower bill than the emperor has.

The emperor penguin's feet are smaller and more completely feathered than the king's. The king doesn't need the extra feathers. It lives north of the emperor in a somewhat milder climate.

Living without flight

Penguins cannot fly. That one fact of penguin life separates them from most other birds. Penguins are simply too big for their wings. Fortunately, penguins really don't need the power of flight.

Birds fly to find food, to escape animals that hunt them, and to travel from one home to another (migrate). Emperor penguins nest and rest on the sea ice. Their food supply is as close as the open sea. They are always within walking distance of open water. Emperors have few enemies in the ocean and even fewer on the ice. And because they are built to withstand the cold, there is no need for them to travel to another home. Everything the emperor needs to survive is close at hand. If the emperor needs to ''explore'' a bit, it climbs on a floating chunk of ice and rides with it. For an emperor penguin, flight is not necessary.

Swimming and diving for food

One of the emperor's needs, naturally, is food. Emperors catch fish and squid by diving. Emperors seem to dive deeper and stay underwater longer than other types of penguins.

The longest recorded dive for an emperor was

eighteen minutes. The usual dive is less than three minutes, however. The record depth for an emperor's plunge is 870 feet (265 m). That may be a record dive for any species of bird! Most emperors dives are less breathtaking, usually in the 65-70 feet (20-21 m) range. The bodies of emperors have special, built-in features that help them dive. For one thing, they have more blood than non-diving birds. Their blood carries more oxygen to help them remain under water. Like any air-breathing animal, they must keep a supply of oxygen in their bloodstream.

An emperor penguin must be a strong, skillful swimmer to catch fish. The emperor uses its webbed feet to help it control direction. But the feet aren't used to move it forward under water. Emperors propel themselves forward through the water with their wings. The

Emperor penguins propel themselves through the water with their wings.

wings are useless for flight in the air, but they are strong and shaped for swimming. Emperor wings are flat and pointed. The front edge is rounded. The back edge is thinner than the front, so the wing moves sharply through the water. The emperor uses its wings together, just as if it were flying through the air. Instead, in a way, it is "flying" through the water at speeds close to fifteen miles per hour (24 km per hour).

Because it has to go underwater to feed, the emperor cannot be light on the waves like a cork. It must be able to dive and swim underwater without too much effort. Many birds that are shallow divers have air sacs, which are pockets of skin that fill with air and help the birds float easily. Air sacs, for instance, help the brown pelican bob to the surface after it dives from the sky. The emperor's only air sacs are its lungs, which, of course, it needs for breathing.

Because it doesn't fly, the emperor penguin has no need for a lightweight, flying frame. Its bones are dense and solid. They also help the emperor sink easily in the water. Still, don't imagine the emperor penguin to be a steel anchor when it hits the sea. It can float without using much effort, but it floats low in the water.

Emperors sometimes travel through the water with so much speed that they can shoot into the air. They coast through the air in a low level leap. Back in the sea, they repeat the leap, all the while moving forward. This mix of swimming and leaping is called "porpoising."

The sea food that emperors eat has a high salt content.

Their bodies cannot use all the salt they take in. To rid themselves of the salt, emperors have glands in the back of their bills. The glands work so well at salt removal that emperors can drink sea water. But they prefer fresh water, which they obtain from eating large amounts of snow.

Getting around on the ice

Emperor penguins are torpedoes in the water. On the ice they are more like barrels. The emperor's fastest waddling speed has been recorded at 1.7 miles per hour

To save energy, emperors usually move very slowly—if at all—while on the ice during winter months.

Penguins seem to enjoy sliding on their stomach feathers. These are Adelie penguins.

(2.8 km per hour). Emperors don't always walk or waddle though. Sometimes they slide across the ice on their stomachs like feathered toboggans. At other times, they don't move at all. Movement requires the use of energy. Emperor penguins have to save their energy, especially during the nesting season. At that time of year, the Antarctic winter, they may be several miles from food, the source of energy. So emperors move as little as possible. An emperor penguin that author Dietland Muller-Schwarze watched at Cape Hallert in Antarctica "stood on the same spot on top of an ice block for twenty-three days."

When young emperors are ready to leave the ice where they were born, they don't have to walk very far. By then it is summer, and the ice breaks up almost under them. Suddenly the sea is at their doorstep.

The typical emperor penguin's entire life is spent at sea level. With few exceptions, emperors are always on fairly level ice. They save energy by having little or no need to climb.

Staying warm, cooling off

Emperor penguins are miracles in temperature control. They live in the coldest region on earth. Yet they must keep their body temperatures at a toasty one hundred degrees Fahrenheit (37° C). They never find air or water temperatures anywhere near their body temperature.

The emperor's problem, then, is how to keep warm in such a horribly cold home. The problem is solved largely by feathers, fat, and form.

The emperor is covered with feathers from head to toe. The emperor and its cousins are more completely feathered than almost any other birds. The emperor has, over most of its body, about seventy feathers per square inch (459 square cm). And the feathers are special. They fit over one another like the tiles on a roof. The downy part at the base of each feather makes up a mat that traps heat. The exposed feathers are oily, so adult emperors are waterproofed.

The underlying feather layer is much like the thick, soft down that comes from eider ducks. Eider down is prized for use in sleeping bags and coats that are to be worn in very cold weather. The "winterized" coat of feathers helps the emperor stay warm in the coldest wind or water. Except for the bill, eyes, and toes, the

This king penguin, like the emperor, is covered with feathers, except for the bill, eyes, and toes.

emperor is completely feathered.

Under the feathers, the emperor has another defense against cold: its fat, or blubber. Fat helps protect the bird's organs. It also gives the emperor a built-in food supply.

In addition to the fat and feathers, the shape of the emperor helps protect it. The emperor is a compact bird. Its body is not really broad or built with long limbs. By being somewhat round and compact, the emperor reduces the amount of flesh on its body surface. Its wing flippers are small and its short legs are tucked under its body.

When male emperors incubate the female's eggs in the middle of the Antarctic winter, they have a special problem. Temperatures drop to nearly 60° below zero Fahrenheit ($-50°$ C). The wind howls at gusts up to 120 miles per hour (192 km per hour). Under these extreme conditions, the emperors fight the cold together. The males huddle together like a team of football players. But while football players gather in a loose circle, emperors pack closely together. Penguins within the huddle expose only a small fraction of their bodies to the wind. By being in the huddle, a penguin reduces its loss of heat. The penguins on the outer edge of the huddle are not nearly as well protected as those in the middle. The birds on the outer rim keep pushing into the huddle. In this way, none of the birds is always on the outside. Each bird, sooner or later, can benefit from the huddle.

Penguins reduce heat loss by huddling together.

Penguins sometimes have to cool off. Their heavy jacket of down makes cooling hard. Most of the time they avoid becoming overheated. By being fairly still when they are on the ice, they save energy and they avoid overheating. But on rare "warm" days, the emperors can ruffle their feathers. That reduces the ability of the feathers to hold heat. It lets air reach more closely to their skin. They also spread their wings, which exposes more of their body surface to the air.

While one penguin dives into the water, another penguin cools itself by spreading its wings.

CHAPTER THREE:

The emperor penguins spend the Antarctic summer at sea and on sea ice. Just exactly where they go "is a puzzle," says Roger Tory Peterson, one of America's best known ornithologists. In the winter, the emperors' nesting season, they gather on the ice which extends from the continent of Antarctica. The groups of emperors are called colonies. The colonies are much easier to find than the scattered emperors at sea. The area where the colonies nest is called a rookery. Emperor rookeries are spread around the Antarctic region.

Adelie penguins live close to emperors, but they do not compete for nesting space. The smaller Adelies, named for a French captain's wife, nest in the summer. They also use ice-free rock slopes along the shores for nesting. The emperor is the only bird to use the Antarctic ice shelves for its rookeries. The species do mix from time to time. Young, non-breeding Adelies and emperors sometimes share a block of floating ice, called an ice floe.

Within the thousands of square miles of their range, emperors pick a variety of places for their rookeries. Some of the emperors nest on very solid ice. Trouble is, the most solid ice is the closest to land. The closer to land, the farther from the sea. And emperors depend on the sea for food. Nevertheless, some emperor rookeries are more than one hundred miles (160 km) from the end of the ice and the start of the open sea.

While emperors need stable ice, they also need ice that will break up in the summer seas. Young emperor penguins are in no shape to walk long distances. They depend on their icy birthplace to break up. That puts them right into the open sea, within easy reach of food.

Emperors also look for places with some natural protection from the hurricanes that sweep down from the high land. They often pick a spot below a hill or ice ledge.

One colony of emperors nests near America's McMurdo Base in Antarctica. That base is well south of the Antarctic circle. McMurdo and other points the same distance from the equator are probably the southern limits for Antarctic penguins. The hottest day ever recorded at McMurdo was 47° Fahrenheit (8.3° C), on January 2, 1974. In winter, during the emperors' nesting season, the temperature averages about minus 13° Fahrenheit ($-25°$ C). The open sea water in that region is about 30° Fahrenheit (about $-1°$ C) all year around.

Emperors are basically birds of the coasts and sea. But on December 31, 1957, a group of Antarctic explorers made a curious discovery. They found footprints in the snow, apparently the tracks of an emperor penguin. They were more than 250 miles (400 km) from the nearest known open water.

Colonies

The emperors begin to gather together in March and April. The exact time depends on the location of the rookery and the weather. March is early autumn in Antarctica.

The penguins do not all show up at the same time. They arrive, often in marching long lines, over a period of about a month. Because they gather in large groups for nesting, emperors are known as ''colonial'' birds. Colonies have different benefits for different birds. In the case of emperors, colonies are important because a large group of birds can crowd together for protection against the cold. Emperor colonies may contain several hundred or, more often, several thousand birds.

Like the emperors, king penguins also gather in large colonies. These kings are on South Georgia Island.

29

Colonial birds, like the emperors, are in a position to learn from each other. They are able to learn such things as the location of food and nesting sites. The colony also means that stray emperor chicks may be able to find foster parents.

The emperors reaching the rookery in March and April are at their greatest weight. They have stuffed themselves with fish, squid, and shrimp. The males especially will need all of their fat reserves. Many of them will go sixteen or eighteen weeks without food.

The rookery is loud, and the smell of thousands of penguins is powerful. But despite the noise and odor, the emperors are calm and content. Emperors are not aggressive penguins, although some of their cousins, such as the kings, are. Emperors cannot afford to waste energy. When males quarrel over a female, the fuss is short lived. If two males duel briefly with their flippers, one quickly backs down.

The colony spends about two months settling itself. Sometimes the penguins locate their old mates. Otherwise, they find new mates.

For years, ornithologists were not sure how emperors could tell males from females. The birds look very much alike. Scientists studying captive emperors at Sea World in San Diego, California, made an important discovery in 1979. They learned that the male emperors have a different rhythm to their call than the females. Both sexes "trumpet" during courtship, and chicks begin trumpeting at the age of six months, when they reach adult size. The scientists found that the length of call differed in the sexes. Any good listener who learns the difference in calls can easily tell the male from the female.

The penguins themselves are very good listeners. They have no trouble picking out possible nesting partners. Their courtship includes calling, bowing, and standing opposite each other with their beaks upright. Finding a mate can take a few hours or a few days. The mating season usually lasts from mid-April to early June.

Dad stays home

The nesting cycle of the emperor penguin is one of the strangest and most fantastic in nature. Not only do emperors nest during the Antarctic winter, they reverse the "normal" nesting roles. Emperor males cannot lay eggs, but they can—and do—incubate the eggs.

Bird eggs must be kept warm until the chick inside is ready to hatch. If the egg becomes cold, the chick inside dies. Therefore, all birds have some means of keeping their eggs warm. The inside of an emperor's egg, for instance, must be kept at about 90° Fahrenheit (32° C). The air temperature may be well over 100° Fahrenheit (37° C) colder than the egg. And the task of keeping the egg warm falls to the male.

The emperor lays one egg. It is rough, greenish-white, and pear-shaped. The egg measures five inches

(13 cm) long. The eggs are usually laid throughout May and incubated for sixty-two to sixty-six days.

Emperors do not build nests. On the ice of Antarctica's coast there is nothing of which to make nests. The emperor, then, must have its ''nest'' built in. As soon as the female lays her egg on the ice, she leaves. The male takes the egg and rolls it onto his feet. He has a fold of skin which extends from his stomach like an apron or pouch. That fold of flesh laps over the egg so that no part of the egg touches the ice. The egg is held fast between the male's feet and lower stomach for two months. The male can hold the egg while using the claws of one foot to scratch his head.

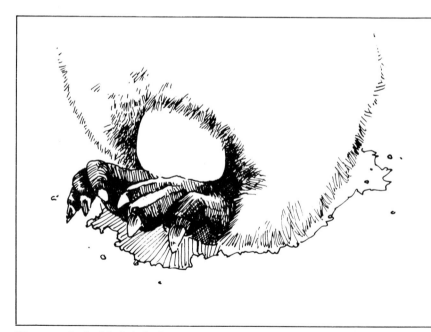

The egg is held tightly between the male's feet, so that the egg never touches the ground.

The male has already spent a month or so at the rookery when the egg arrives. Now he has another two months of duty before he can leave the rookery and dive for food. But the male is in no hurry to leave. His urge to incubate is very strong. If his egg is broken through an accident, he may try to incubate a piece of ice in its place!

While the male incubates the egg, the female feeds. She has left the rookery to return to open water. The distance between the rookery and open water has increased since she arrived for nesting. The colder days have made more ice. Her hike may take her more than one hundred miles (160 km) across the ice fields. Her job now is to fatten up and bring food back for her chick when it hatches.

She has gone perhaps six weeks without food. She is not as heavily blubbered as her mate, and she has the added stress of producing an egg. That one egg may weigh up to one and one-quarter pounds (.6 kg)! When she leaves the rookery, she may have lost nearly forty percent of her previous weight. She is in no condition to spend another two months without food. That is why the male remains behind and the female goes for food.

Meanwhile, the male emperors are living very slow lives in the almost total darkness of June and July, midwinter in Antarctica. For nearly six weeks, there is no sun. When blizzards whirl across the ice, the wind makes it seem like 150° Fahrenheit below zero ($-100°$ C).

Despite the egg on his feet, the male penguin can

move. On fair weather days, a male may wander as much as a mile. He doesn't move quickly, but he can hobble about and still hold the egg. Sometimes an egg does get broken. The emperor males need to be able to move, even if it is just to huddle with other males, when the cold and wind become overpowering.

The males undergo quite a change during their fatherhood. Four months may pass between their arrival at the rookery and the time the females return. During that time, the males are without food. The male has a heavy layer of blubber on which he lives. Each male may lose half his body weight before he feeds again. An unlucky few will starve to death.

Help on the way

The females begin to return to the rookery about the time that their eggs hatch. Nature's timing is remarkable, but not always perfect. The chick may hatch before the female's return, usually in July and August. If the female is late, the male can feed the chick for a short time. He can bring up a liquid food from his throat.

Very few people have seen the return of female emperors from their fishing trips. There is some question about whether they locate their mates or go to any male which is willing to give up its chick. It seems that some females do locate their mates by calling. Others probably take over a chick from any available male.

As the females return, they take up the duty of keeping the chick warm. The chicks are hatched during the worst blizzards of the year. They must be kept warm or they will die. There is no sunshine at this time of year. The days are almost total darkness. No other bird enters the world in such terrible conditions.

The mother penguin keeps the chick on her feet and protects it with a flap of her lower stomach, just as the male did. Meanwhile, the hungry males begin their journey across the ice to open water.

The female has brought about seven pounds (3 kg) of partly digested sea food in her. That food, which she will regurgitate for the chick, will last about a month. By then the male will have returned from his feeding trip to the sea, so he can feed the chick.

Penguins feed their chicks by regurgitating into their mouths.

Raising junior emperors

Raising a young emperor is a very hard job for the parents. Yet emperor chicks must be born in the winter. They become large birds, and they take more than five months to grow up. If they were born in the brief Antarctic summer, it would be winter by the time they had grown up. Then they would be a long way from the sea because of the increasing amount of ice. They would not be able to walk to the sea, as their parents can, because they would not be fat enough yet. The parents would never have been able to feed them enough to make them fat. By being born in mid-winter, the chicks reach adulthood as the ice is breaking up. The open sea is moving closer to shore and the rookery. That means the young birds can reach food easily. It also means that as their appetite grows, the parents find the sea easier to reach for food.

Emperor chicks are born with only a light covering of down on their bodies. Their heads are feathered, because they will stick out from under the parents' warm belly flap. The chicks' bodies are kept warm by the parents' feathers. During this time, the chicks are noisy. Their calls in this cold, dark wilderness are music to some ears. One writer described their notes as the "sweetest natural sound in Antarctica."

After six weeks of life in its parents' pouches, the chick tumbles into the "outdoors." It gets too big for the parents to hold. And it has enough feathers on its body to resist the cold. But the chick doesn't go off by itself. It huddles together with other chicks. When the parents return from fishing trips, they pick out their own chicks by voice.

Emperor chicks are very attractive. They have black "caps" and white circles around each eye. Their bodies are silver gray and a white band runs under their chins. The white may help parents locate them in the darkness.

As the chicks age, winter begins to loosen its grip. The parents take turns making feeding trips to the ocean. In August, the sun begins to rise again each day. The ice slowly melts.

The ice near the rookeries usually breaks up in late December or January, summer in Antarctica. The young emperors should have adult feathers by then. But if the ice breaks up early, the chicks will still be downy. Down gives them little protection against the sea, so they will drown. Late-born chicks face the same problem; they may not have had time to grow the feathers that will protect them against water.

In normal years the chicks are able to ride ice floes out to sea. When they float away from the rookery, they look much like their parents. In another eighteen months they will look exactly like the adults. They will be ready for their nesting at some time between the ages of four and eight years.

Life and death

Not all emperor chicks survive to ride the ice out to sea. Some are lost before they hatch. The shuffling about of the males can lead to broken eggs. Stray chicks are sometimes fought over by adults without chicks of their own. As adults tug at the chick in a penguin tug-of-war, the chick may be torn to pieces.

The greatest threats to young emperors are blizzards, falling ice, and deep cracks in the ice. Young emperors that wander away from the group are the most likely to die.

Few animals bother the emperor rookeries. A bird called the giant fulmar takes some emperor chicks. Sheathbills, skuas, and giant petrels, three other bird predators, take a few eggs and small chicks. But they are minor problems compared to the weather.

Because they are so large, emperor penguins have few natural enemies.

All species of penguins are probably safer on land and ice than at sea. Adult emperors have no enemies on the ice. Once at sea, they are not as safe. Killer whales feed on emperors from time to time. Leopard seals, large, fierce Antarctic predators, take some emperors in the sea also.

Fitting into the ecosystem

Like every other place on earth, the Antarctic region has its own plants and animals. The plants and animals depend on one another in many ways. Together they form a community of living things. Each plant and animal has a role, or "job." As long as each species can do its "job," the community works well. This community of natural things is sometimes called an ecosystem.

A basic part of the Antarctic ecosystem is a group of marine plants called phytoplankton. They use sunlight and materials in the sea for their food. These tiny plants are food for krill. Krill are small, too, but much larger than the phytoplankton. Krill are shrimp-like animals. The emperors live mostly on fish and squid which eat the krill. In turn, emperors sometimes are meals for the killer whales and leopard seals. Meanwhile, the penguins, through their waste, return some food particles to the sea. The waste becomes food for marine plants. (The auk family in the Northern seas has a similar role.)

CHAPTER FOUR:

Some penguins were known to Europeans after Magellan's voyage in 1520. "Strange geese," he called them. But the emperor penguins were unknown to anyone until 1820. No one lived in the Antarctic, and few sailing ships came anywhere near it. Finally, in December, 1820, Thaddeus von Bellinghausen caught an emperor. In 1844, the species was written about by an English scientist, G.R. Gray. Gray studied emperors brought to Europe by the James Clark Ross expedition of 1839-1843.

The emperor's scientific name, *Aptenodytes forsteri*, honors two Germans, Johann R. Forster and his son. The Forsters traveled to the Southern seas with James Cook (1772-1775). They saw king penguins, but probably not emperors. Many years later, Gray looked at their drawings and thought they showed emperors. So the Forsters, for a time, were credited with having discovered emperors. However, the Forsters' written descriptions of the penguins makes it clear that they had seen king penguins.

The first emperor rookery was found in October, 1902, by the Scott expedition. It was very obvious to the men that the emperors must have nested during the winter. They were amazed!

In late June, 1911, three men led by Edward Wilson made an incredible trip back to that colony. The trip took them seventy miles (112 km) each way by foot. They traveled a total of thirty-six days, hauling sleds behind them. One day the temperature reached minus 77° Fahrenheit (−60° C).

Near the penguin colony, at Cape Crozier, the three men built a hut of stones and covered it with a canvas. They made a short visit to the rookery and killed three emperors for their blubber. They used the fat to light their stove. They also took a half dozen eggs for study. They were unable to make a second visit to the rookery. Hurricane winds pounded their rock shelter for seven days. Dragging themselves over ice ridges in the Antarctic darkness, they reached Cape Evans and safety in early August. Apsley Cherry-Garrard, one of the three men, wrote a book in 1922, about their trip. He called it *The Worst Journey in the World.* Now the Cape Crozier rookery can be reached in thirty minutes by helicopter from the McMurdo Base in Antarctica.

A second emperor colony was discovered in 1912, at Haswell Island. The third emperor colony was not

King penguins were discovered in the 1770's, by two Germans, Johann Forster and his son. At first, the men thought they had found emperors.

found until 1948. But since 1950, more than thirty emperor rookeries have been mapped. The largest, on Coulman Island, has over 100,000 emperors. Antarctic explorers are still busy, and more emperor colonies may be discovered.

Out of harm's way

There is an advantage to living on the far end of the earth. The emperor has remained undiscovered, while other kinds of penguins to the north were being hunted for their skins and blubber. Their skins were used for

Because of their frozen homeland, Adelie and emperor penguins were almost never bothered by people.

clothing, shoes, caps, floor mats, and even local roofing. More were killed for the oil that came from their boiled fat. Penguin eggs were collected, too.

The emperor's population has never been threatened by people. Even if anyone had wanted to take emperors, the price of reaching them in their frozen retreat would have been too great. Today, penguins of all species are protected.

Emperors in captivity

Penguins are hard to keep in captivity. It's hard for zoos to make a home anything like the one that wild penguins enjoy. Antarctic species like the emperor are especially hard to raise.

But Sea World in San Diego has done remarkably well with emperors. Sea World's emperors, along with other species, are kept in a cold, icy environment. The temperature never rises above freezing. In the public viewing area, the penguins have a man-made ice shelf that is covered each day with twelve thousand pounds (5,400 kg) of crushed ice. Beyond the ice is a seven and one-half foot (2.3 m) deep pool. The water temperature is kept at 45° Fahrenheit (7° C). The exhibit is indeed a little Antarctica. Sea World's exhibit was named the best new zoo exhibit of 1983.

There is more to the project than meets the eye. The

Sea World penguin building is also a place for ornithologists to study penguin habits. It is also a place where, for the first time in a zoo, emperor penguins can act much as they do in the Antarctic. The first hatching of an emperor chick in captivity took place in 1980, and several more emperors have been born in captivity since that time.

Many of the emperors being raised at Sea World should have long lives. Captive emperors in less ideal homes have lived to the age of thirty-four. No one really knows how long wild emperors live.

The emperor's future

The Antarctic is home for about 300,000 emperor penguins. They have never been bothered very much by man. There are probably about the same number of emperors today as when von Bellinghausen found the species in 1820. The emperor is safe for now.

In the future, it may not be as secure. Mankind's need for more food will surely take us to the Antarctic seas. More and more of the krill eaten by seals, penguins, and fish may some day be needed by people. The emperors may have to share their food supply. If that happens, the number of emperors will probably decrease.

In the meantime, life for the emperor penguin remains as it has been for thousands upon thousands of years.

For thousands of years, the life of the emperor penguin has remained the same.

Antarctica

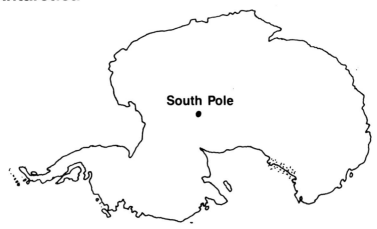

South Pole

The emperor penguin has been seen in most regions along the coastal waters of Antarctica. One area mentioned in our book is America's McMurdo Base which is designated with the shaded area.

INDEX/GLOSSARY:

47

WILDLIFE
HABITS & HABITAT

READ AND ENJOY THE SERIES:

If you would like to know more about all kinds of wildlife, you should take a look at the other books in this series.

You'll find books on bald eagles and other birds. Books on alligators and other reptiles. There are books about deer and other big-game animals. And there are books about sharks and other creatures that live in the ocean.

In all of the books you will learn that life in the wild is not easy. But you will also learn what people can do to help wildlife survive. So read on!

ABB-3878

JUL 28 1989